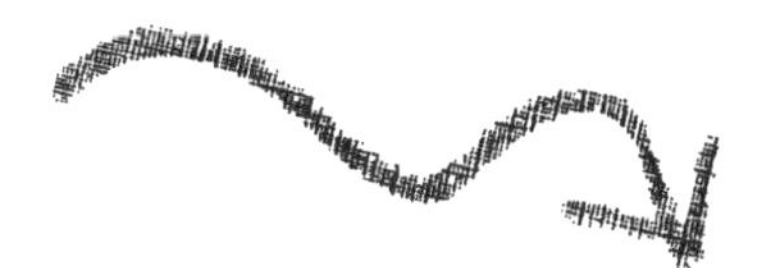

TABLE OF CONTENTS

HOW TO USE THIS BOOK

- BEFORE YOU START WRITING -

1. Take a minute to look through the eight genres and decide which one excites you the most.
2. Read through the story prompts in that genre and choose the one that "pops" out at you the most. Usually it's the one that you can imagine the quickest.

AWESOME! LET'S MOVE ON TO THE CHARACTERS!

- CHARACTERS -

1. Picture each character.
2. What are each of them wearing?
3. Do they have accents or use a favorite saying?
4. What does each character want? Money? Fame? Save someone? Escape from a villain?

GOOD JOB! LET'S MOVE ON TO TIME PERIOD AND LOCATION!

- TIME PERIOD AND LOCATION -

1. Is the time period today? The future? The past?
2. Are they on this planet? Another planet? In outer space?
3. What technology is available to your characters?
4. What's the weather like? Are the seasons different than ours?
5. How do they get around? Walking? Bikes and cars? Spaceships? Teleporting?!?

That's it! You're ready to get to writing on your story. Remember, this is your story.

Bonus: If your story is longer than the two pages in the genre section, just flip to the back where there are 10 extra pages to continue your story!

Start writing and have fun!

REALISTIC FICTION

Emma was born a little different, enough different that her parents kept her out of school until now. She wants nothing more than to be accepted and to blend in with her class-mates. One more dilemma is that her brother Aiden is just a year younger and is nervous about her return to their school as well.

Ethan just moved up to the big leagues. At least that's what his parents told him when they enrolled him in a private school. They see opportunity. He sees starting over with no friends and new surroundings. Making matters worse, he can't keep his eyes off of Olivia, the most popular girl in school, and her jock boyfriend Dylan has noticed.

REALISTIC FICTION

Making the cheer squad is the only thing on Hannah's mind. Well, that and Zachary. The problem is her best friend Grace has her eyes set on Zachary and called "dibs." Hannah is stuck. Zachary or Grace. Can she keep her friendship intact if she wants both?

REALISTIC FICTION

Mia and her dad live on the road, literally. He's a long-haul truck driver and is doing his best to homeschool her, well, truck school her if you want to be accurate. Mia's grandparents offered to have her stay with them and go to school, but that would mean leaving her father and only seeing him a couple of days a week. She want's some normalcy in her life and more than anything to make friends. How does she tell him she's ready to "park it" at her grandparent's house?

REALISTIC FICTION

Everyone wants a best friend. It's natural. Caden's best friend is Olivia. Having a girl as a best friend is trouble enough without finding out she is a self-proclaimed psychic. Now the teasing and whispering at school is relentless. Caden tried to reason with Olivia, but she won't stop talking about her psychic abilities. What's worse is she keeps getting things right.

REALISTIC FICTION

Ella knows two things for sure; her brother Noah sneaks out every night and her parents don't know. When Ella confronts Noah he tells her to "mind her own business" and "it's for the good of the family." Unsatisfied, Ella decides to follow Noah one night and is surprised by what she discovers.

HISTORICAL FICTION

Charles was 13-years old when World War 2 started. Rumors rumbled throughout his small town in Montana, but the war seemed far away. Until one day when his older brother surprised them all and joined the military, leaving Charles and his single mom to fend for themselves. With his brother gone and his mother struggling to put food on the table, Charles is forced to step up and take his brother's place and fight against the anger he was feeling when his brother abandoned them.

HISTORICAL FICTION

Bella grew up in a small town where the most exciting thing that ever happened was when the neighbor's cow somehow ended up in their living room. David moved into town and quickly took a liking to Bella, but her parents just as quickly took a disliking to him. David is caught by Bella's father in the tree outside her window with a necklace belonging to Bella's mother. Bella has to decide whether to believe David's story or face the possible truth.

HISTORICAL FICTION

The summer of 1968 started out awesome for Gary. With a fresh driver's license in his pocket and the keys to his father's old pickup truck, he and his best friend Mark were headed to the beach for the weekend. Camping on the beach, the two drifted off only to wake up and find the truck gone, along with their wallets. With no money and no truck, the two set off on a 200-mile journey home.

HISTORICAL FICTION

Being an apprentice in 1776 was a fortunate blessing for Nicolas and his family. Not every young man was lucky enough to be offered training to become a boat builder. His parents were required to pay a substantial amount to enroll him under a master crafts-man. On his first day, Nicolas ran into Joseph, the lead apprentice who didn't appreciate how quickly Nicolas took to their craft. Besides the hard work and long hours, Nicolas has to find a way to deal with Joseph without losing his apprenticeship and shaming his family.

Annie feels abandoned. Her father put her on a train to go live with a family friend while he goes to work for the railroad. She arrives a week later only to find the house vacant. With her father miles away and no money for the return trip, Annie decides to stay at the abandoned home and find a way to support herself until her father arrives.

HISTORICAL FICTION

The spray of the ocean stung Hamilton's face as he fought to keep his balance on the ship's churning deck. His parents were below deck fighting seasickness and had warned him to not stray above deck. His family's 1892 voyage to America was exciting and terrifying all at once. A wave crashed against the ship's hull and knocked Hamilton off his feet and sent him careening toward the rail.

MYSTERY

Lily's father, an estate attorney, is missing a client's will from his office. If the will isn't found, the client's inheritance will be turned over to his fiance, instead of deserving relatives and friends who were promised inheritances. Making matters worse, some of her friends are whispering that her father was involved. With her dog Buster, Lily sets off to find the will and exonerate her father.

MYSTERY

When the school principal, Mr. Hodges, comes up missing, rumors start swirling about why he left and even if he was abducted. Austin goes to Mr. Hodges's house and finds his car in the driveway and the front door unlocked. He pushes the door open and is shocked by what he finds.

MYSTERY

Emilia lives in a small town where everyone knows everyone else's business. When a lawman comes to town and accuses Emilia's father of murder, she has to do everything she can to find the real killer and set her father free.

MYSTERY

Hunter took a long swig of his drink and laughed as his best friend Brandon blew bubbles into his own drink. A loud thump at another table grabbed their attention as a man fell to the ground holding his chest. Hunter watched as a man in a dark ballcap quickly grabbed a glass from the man's table and sprinted out the door.

MYSTERY

Maya and Jasmine are twins. They think alike, dress alike, and even talk alike. When a trophy at the school goes missing from the display case a secret witness claims that one of them did it. Now it's up to them to prove their innocence and find the trophy.

MYSTERY

A stranger comes to town at the same time the bank is robbed. Elijah saw the man leaving the bank just before it was robbed, only the man he saw was wearing brown dress shoes instead of the cowboy boots he now had on.

SCIENCE FICTION

Jack and Logan find a website advertising for "Astronauts Wanted – no experience necessary" on the homepage. Jack dares Logan to answer the ad and contact the webpage owner, Dr. Barker. To their surprise, Dr. Barker responds back and agrees to meet. The boys are shocked to learn that Dr. Barns is a former NASA employee who was forced into retirement for his hair-brained ideas about turning recycled bottles into space ships.

SCIENCE FICTION

An army of mind-controlled baboons is taking over the government. Each baboon is implanted with a mini-processor enabling the baboons to speak, but also enabling its creator, Dr. Chambers, to control the baboons. While Dr. Chambers focuses her baboons on the adults, Riley Ramsfield and her dog Shotskie work to foil the plot and save the world.

SCIENCE FICTION

Leonard is a skinny kid who gets teased, a lot. He spends most of his days after school wandering through the woods behind his house. After an exceptionally difficult day of getting bullied at school, he goes for another walk in the woods and discovers a small spacecraft. He builds up the courage to touch the outer hull of the spaceship when a door whooshes open and a miniature purple alien greets him.

SCIENCE FICTION

Ava wants more than anything to follow in her father's footsteps and Captain an Explorer Class space vessel. She wakes up one morning and heads off to class in the lower decks of the ship, just like every other day. Only when she arrives she finds the other students and no adults. They've vanished from the ship. Ava's wishes to become Captain have come true, though not in the way she had hoped, and now she is left to run the ship and search for her father and the other adults.

SCIENCE FICTION

Kayla and Luke have been best friends for as long as they can remember. Though it's no surprise since their families are the only ones living on Mondox. Their planet is on the outermost ring of the Federated Planet Continuum (FPC). When a distress signal reaches her personal computing pad in her room, Kayla convinces Luke to take her family's travel pod and investigate.

SCIENCE FICTION

Jayden and his younger brother Gabriel have a normal life. A mother. A father. A dog. Only, something doesn't feel right. While cooking up a snack on the stove, Jayden gets distracted and burns his hand. He runs some cold water over his fingertips and the skin comes off, revealing a silver robotic skeleton underneath.

SCIENCE FICTION

Justin and his family are watching his younger brother's football team. In the middle of the game, a spacecraft lands on the football field. A hatch opens and reveals a tall, thin greyish being. The being scans the crowd and then points directly at Justin and says, "Justin Walker, come forth and no one else gets harmed." Justin stands and heads toward the craft.

FANTASY

Ariana is a Bansha. You would never know except for the fact that she has four fingers on each hand. But what others don't see or know is that she has the ability to read minds. Her ability has led her to discover that the King is rounding up others like her and forcing them to use their abilities to do his bidding and control his kingdom. Ariana has to find a way to avoid detection and to free those being held against their will.

FANTASY

Makayla stared out her bedroom window at the moving van across the street. She watched as an elderly woman on the porch directed the men unloading the van as to where the items go in the house. Next to the woman was a red and blue lawn gnome. As Makayla watches, the hat on the gnome's head topples off onto the porch and the gnome picks it up and puts it back on his head.

FANTASY

Hermax wasn't afraid of war. He hoped that one day when he grew older he would be considered to join Lord Ephoros's royal guard. For now, he was nothing more than chamber servant, though he had done his duties well enough to now serve Lord Ephoros's younger brother, Lord Anthos. Just before entering Anthos's chambers, Hermax hears the younger brother plotting to kill Ephoros.

FANTASY

Windshone knew that becoming a wizard wasn't a choice, it was a calling. The calling came in the form of a star on the inner-wrist and appeared on the recipient's 13th birthday. Most importantly, the star never appeared on a girl, until now.

FANTASY

Dwarves were miners. Lud knew that. He had many generations before him to prove that he was born to be a miner. Lud finished his regular day's work and retreated to an abandoned tunnel where he was following a thin vein of gold in his spare time. Raising his hammer, he struck at the black wall of rock and an explosion of stone landed at his feet. He looked down and saw a wand at his feet.

FANTASY

While visiting her aged aunt, Tatiana searches for a pen to write her aunt a note when she stumbles upon a red ruby in a desk drawer. Picking up the rock she turns to see her aunt watching her. Her aunt explains that the rock is a portal to any time period she wants to see. All she has to do is hold the rock and say the exact date and time where she wants to go. The only hitch is that any time she spends in the portal takes off twice the time of her real life.

FANTASY

All Dodfast ever wanted was to be a Dragonrider. When he asked his father if he could attend the Zarsi Dragonrider Academy, his father shook his head and reminded Dodfast that he was a hobbit. Frustrated, Dodfast went for a walk near the Ardland's where he climbed the rocky face of the jagged hills. Sitting near the top of one of the crests, he closed his eyes and took in a deep breath. A cracking sound behind him caught his attention and he turned to see a dragon's egg with a thin line running across it and resting in a crag in the rocks.

ACTION/ADVENTURE

Ryan could hardly sleep. The thought of traveling with his father to a remote Alaskan
village in his father's bush plane was something he had been waiting for his whole life.
Halfway through their trip, the plane's prop stalled and his father was forced to crash
land the plane in the middle of the woods. With his father unconscious, Ryan is forced to
abandon him and fight the wilderness to find help and rescue his father.

ACTION/ADVENTURE

During a field trip to the Smithsonian's Natural History Museum, Mia was drawn to an exhibition that was roped off to the public. On the ground, just beyond the edge of the exhibit's platform was a small stone with a leather loop running through a hole in the middle. Mia reached down to pick it up and the leather strands quickly wrapped around her wrist and fastened itself into a knot.

Jose crouched behind the stack of boxes on the peer and watched as the men loaded the boat in the darkness. With his parents missing, the only clues to where they had been taken led Jose to the man now standing on the upper deck of the boat. Jose waited for his chance to stow away on the boat and get some answers.

Mackenzie's mother was desperate to earn the extra money needed for her and Mackenzie to keep their house. The only alternative was to rent a room to make up the difference. A man with a Russian accent was the only person that applied and Mackenzie's mother quickly accepted. The first few days were fine. Then Mackenzie discovered the man was a spy.

Isaac was infatuated with numbers. His father even bought him a book about ciphers, basically a set of steps to encrypt and decrypt messages. Isaac discovered a set of numbers scribbled on a wall at an abandoned warehouse just outside of town. Three sets of numbers. He decrypted the first set easy enough, "HELP ME." He finally recognized the second and third set of numbers. They were map coordinates.

ACTION/ADVENTURE

Jenna couldn't believe her parents let her go on the trip with her best friend's family. A once-in-a-lifetime visit to the Swiss Alps. Ready to climb and explore, Jenna and Sofia set off at a pace to keep ahead of Sofia's parents and her younger brother. Finally out of sight, the girls heard a rumbling sound and watched in horror as an avalanche of snow filled the area between them and Sofia's family.

Of all the things Cadence could be called, normal was not one of them. In fact, she prided herself on finding ways to do things easier and more efficiently than everyone else, even if it meant the other kids laughed at her. But things started to change when she met Eric.

Adam had two different colored eyes. Really. A blue one and a brown one. His mom said that one represented her side of the family and one for his father's side of the family. Actually, that was nothing compared to the other thing no one ever saw.

Brooklyn was the most clumsy cheerleader anyone had ever seen. In fact, the cheer coach wouldn't let her do any stunts with the other cheerleaders, "Even if they were covered in pillows." Brooklyn's goal was to finally make it to the top of the "human pyramid" stunt one day. She had a grand scheme to get there.

Abby had finally made it to the big leagues. She was on track to be the class president. The only thing holding her back was her brother who had just turned old enough to go to her school. To make matters worse, he was the worst prankster in the world.

COMEDY/HUMOR

Mr. Barrett was your typical, self-proclaimed nerd. He loved everything about science and even had a pocket-protector for his stack of pens and pencils. When Wyatt started school he was forced to take Mr. Barrett's science class. Not a big deal, except Mr. Barrett was Wyatt's father.

COMEDY/HUMOR

Tristan told a lie. In the grand scheme of things, it wasn't that big of a lie. After all, it was only numbers. He applied for an online job and put down that he was 32 years old. Guess what? He got the job. Now he's leading a double life.

HORROR

Addison knew better than to go into the mine. Her parents had warned her over and over again. Standing at the entrance, Addison thought she heard a voice inside. She called back, but nothing. As she turned to leave, the voice called out again. Addison paused, then turned on the light on her cellphone and crept into the opening of the mine.

HORROR

Cooper was annoyed at having to walk Ms. Mayfield's dog. The little chihuahua was loud and sometimes nipped at Cooper's heels. Cooper's mother insisted that he help out Ms. Mayfield after she had gone through hip surgery. Cooper grumbled as he walked the dog and tugged on the leash when it stopped to bark at the vacant house at the end of the block. Then the dogged lurched forward and pulled and the leash from Cooper's hand and ran into the ghoulish home.

HORROR

Carson followed the yells of his younger sister from the back of the neighbor's house. As he turned the corner, he could hear a buzzing sound growing louder and louder. His sister was wedged against the far corner of the yard. In front of her was a baseball-sized wasp readying itself to strike.

HORROR

It was a dare. It was a dare by a popular girl, which made it worse. Faith claimed to not be afraid of anything, but the only way to prove it was to spend the night in the Castle House, an abandoned mansion where the Castle family was killed. Legend had it that the Castle family were ghosts and stuck in the home for eternity. After talking her best friend Destiny into joining her, the two set off to confront the legend.

HORROR

"Nobody goes into the car cemetery after dark." That's what everyone said. Xavier wasn't "nobody" and set out to prove it to everyone else. With his cellphone in his pocket to take picture-proof of having been there at night, Xavier set out to prove the other chickens wrong. He decided to sit inside one of the junked-out cars and take a selfie. Xavier made his way to the middle of the wrecked cars and chose a rusted out truck. As he creaked open the car door open, a hand slid out from under the car and grabbed his ankle.

HORROR

The boys laughed as they told stories around the campfire. When it was Devin's turn, he squinted his eyes and stared into the glow of the fire. A boy snickered but quickly quieted. Devin continued and began to share the tale of the Wookalar, a half-man half-boar with tusks protruding from the corners of his mouth. A loud grunt sounded in the woods just outside the fire's casted light, followed by a piercing squeal.

FREE WRITE/CONTINUE STORY

FREE WRITE/CONTINUE STORY

FREE WRITE/CONTINUE STORY

FREE WRITE/CONTINUE STORY

FREE WRITE/CONTINUE STORY

FREE WRITE/CONTINUE STORY

FREE WRITE/CONTINUE STORY